D1710573

Why *Voting* Matters

Why Should People Vote?

Kristen Rajczak Nelson

PowerKiDS press

NEW YORK

Published in 2019 by The Rosen Publishing Group, Inc.
29 East 21st Street, New York, NY 10010

Editor: Elizabeth Krajnik
Book Design: Rachel Rising

Photo Credits: Cover Hero Images/Getty Images; Cover, pp. 1, 3, 4, 6, 8, 10, 12, 14, 16, 18, 20, 22, 23, 24 (background) PepinoVerde/Shutterstock.com; pp. 5, 11, 19 Hill Street Studios/Blend Images/Getty Images; p. 7 https://commons.wikimedia.org/wiki/File:Declaration_of_Independence_(1819),_by_John_Trumbull.jpg; p. 9 Rena Schild/Shutterstock.com; p. 13 Drew Angerer/Getty Images News/Getty Images; p. 15 Mark Makela/Getty Images News/Getty Images; p. 17 Marjorie Kamys Cotera/Bob Daemmrich Photography/Alamy; p. 21 Bloomberg//Getty Images; p. 22 Ariel Skelley/DigitalVision/Getty Images.

Library of Congress Cataloging-in-Publication Data

Names: Rajczak Nelson, Kristen, author.
Title: Why should people vote? / Kristen Rajczak Nelson.
Description: New York : PowerKids Press, 2019. | Series: Why voting matters | Includes index.
Identifiers: LCCN 2017054407| ISBN 9781538330234 (library bound) | ISBN 9781538330258 (pbk.) | ISBN 9781538330265 (6 pack)
Subjects: LCSH: Voting--United States--Juvenile literature. | Political participation--United States--Juvenile literature.
Classification: LCC JK1978 R356 2019 | DDC 324.60973--dc23
LC record available at https://lccn.loc.gov/2017054407

Manufactured in the United States of America

CPSIA Compliance Information: Batch #CS18PK For further information contact Rosen Publishing, New York, New York at 1-800-237-9932.

Contents

A Job to Do

The U.S. government is made up of many people, many of whom have been **elected** to their jobs. U.S. **citizens** have the right to vote, which gives them a job, too. They have to choose these government leaders. It's important that citizens do this job, just like leaders need to do theirs!

5

As Colonists

When the United States was a British **colony**, the colonists had little say in British government. That was one reason they fought for their freedom. The Founding Fathers wanted to make sure citizens would be heard in the new nation. They didn't want one person to have all the power.

Votes for All

Today, the U.S. **Constitution** gives most citizens over 18 years old the right to vote. No matter how much money someone has or what their race or faith is, everyone's vote is equal. Anyone who can vote should do so because the government needs to hear from all kinds of people.

9

Representing the People

Government leaders **represent** people from towns, counties, districts, and states. In order to be elected, they need to listen to the people they want to represent. People can let these leaders know what their beliefs and values are by voting. Voters also let their representatives know their thoughts by calling, emailing, or writing to them.

Votes Show Favor

Voters often show **support** for an idea, law, or a leader by voting. Even if the leader doesn't win or the law isn't passed, voters show their support by taking time to cast a vote. If enough people show support, the person or law might be considered again later.

13

Asking for Change

Voting for or against a leader or law can send another message, too. Voters may ask for change! If a leader doesn't do what they promised, voters can vote for someone else in the next election. A group of voters might support someone who has new ideas they agree with.

Elections Affect All

The outcome of an election can affect how schools are run, how the government spends its money, and even how clean the streets are. In order to have a say in these matters, citizens need to vote. Local leaders affect the people who live in the area they represent. National leaders affect everyone living in the United States!

MY VOTE WILL BE
MY VOICE

MI VOTO SERÁ
MI VOZ

17

Popular Vote

There are millions of voters in the United States. In most elections, each voter has one vote that is counted as part of the popular vote. The popular vote is the total amount of votes cast in an election. Most elections are decided by the popular vote. That means each person's vote is important!

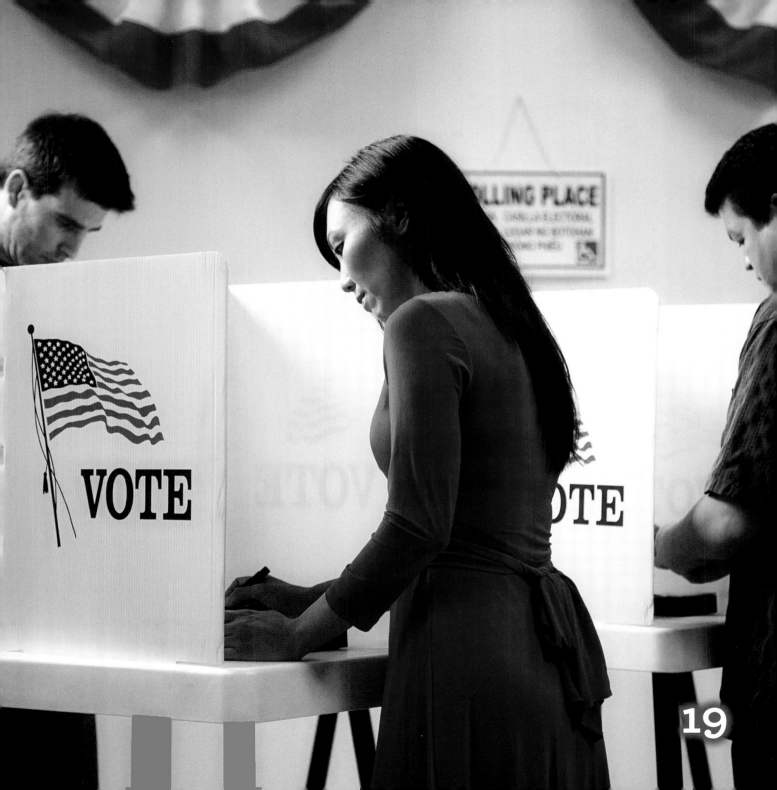

19

The Electoral College

The U.S. president isn't elected by popular vote. When citizens vote for president, they are voting for a person called an elector who will vote for them as part of the **Electoral College**. Each state has a number of votes in the Electoral College based on its population, or the number of people living there.

ELECTORAL COLLEGE MA
MA
RI 4
CT 7
NJ 15
DE 3
MD 10
DC 3
R ME IN!
IRREGULARTIMES.COM
NH 4
VT 3
MA 12
RI 4
CT 7
NJ 15
DE 3
MD 10
DC 3
ME IN!
IRREGULARTIMES.COM

Voters' Voices

No one is forced to vote, and many people choose not to. The more people who vote, the more likely it is that citizens' voices will be heard! Leaders know who is voting and tend to work harder for groups that turn out to vote. If people don't vote, they're letting others decide what's best for them!

Glossary

citizen: A person who lives in a country and has the rights given to them by that country's laws.

colony: An area that is controlled by or belongs to a country and is usually far away from it. Someone who lives in a colony is a colonist.

constitution: The basic laws by which a country, state, or group is governed.

elect: To choose someone for a position, especially in government, by voting.

Electoral College: A body of 538 electors who cast votes to elect the president and vice president.

represent: To act officially for someone or something.

support: The act of showing you agree with someone or something.

Index

Websites

Due to the changing nature of Internet links, PowerKids Press has developed an online list of websites related to the subject of this book. This site is updated regularly. Please use this link to access the list: www.powerkidslinks.com/wvm/wspv